T0375475

THE LOST 13 TRIBES OF ISRAEL

GOD'S LETTER OF DIVORCE

JOHAN ANDREAS RAUTENBACH

WESTBOW
PRESS®
A DIVISION OF THOMAS NELSON
& ZONDERVAN

WestBow Press books may be ordered through booksellers or by contacting:

WestBow Press
A Division of Thomas Nelson & Zondervan
1663 Liberty Drive
Bloomington, IN 47403
www.westbowpress.com
844-714-3454

Because of the dynamic nature of the Internet, any web addresses or
links contained in this book may have changed since publication and
may no longer be valid. The views expressed in this work are solely those
of the author and do not necessarily reflect the views of the publisher,
and the publisher hereby disclaims any responsibility for them.

All Scripture quotations are taken from the King James Version, public domain.

Any people depicted in stock imagery provided by Getty Images are
models, and such images are being used for illustrative purposes only.
Certain stock imagery © Getty Images.

ISBN: 979-8-3850-2053-9 (sc)
ISBN: 979-8-3850-2054-6 (e)

Library of Congress Control Number: 2024904717

Print information available on the last page.

WestBow Press rev. date: 03/04/2024

THE MEANING OF THE NAMES
OF HOSEA'S CHILDREN

In Revelation 19:7-9, it talks about the Bride of Christ, symbolized as someone wearing clean and white fine linen. This fine linen represents the righteousness of the saints, meaning the goodness and purity of believers.

Now, there's a question about whether the Bride of Christ is the same as the people of Israel in the Old and New Testaments. They seem to be wearing the same clothing and doing similar things. Some wonder if the Church has replaced Israel, but the idea is that God doesn't play games with words. However, due to negative changes in Israel's behavior, God issued a letter of divorce, as mentioned in Jeremiah 3:8. This doesn't mean they won't be God's children, but they won't be known as God's wife anymore.

This concept is illustrated in the Old Testament through the prophet Hosea. Hosea married a woman with a troubled past (referred to as a "whore" in the text), and their children were given symbolic names:

Jezreel
Lo-ruhamah
Lo-ammi

These names and the story of Hosea help demonstrate the relationship between God and Israel, highlighting the consequences of their actions. The Old Testament promises that, despite the change in the relationship, Israel will still be known as God's children. This provides a tangible example for anyone, including children, to understand the concept of God's relationship with His people.

Jezreel

Jezreel refers to the valley where Israel's letter of divorce took effect. This valley is significant because the break in relations between God and Israel occurred there. In the future, the return to God by Israel is prophesied to happen at the same place, now known as Armageddon (Revelation 16:16). Armageddon is associated with the hill of Megiddo and the Jezreel Valley. Despite the letter of divorce, God never forgot Israel. The Northern tribes (Israel) and the Jews (Judah) went through periods of separation, symbolized by Assyria and Babylon, respectively. Hosea's act of buying back his wife, Gomer, represents God's eventual reconciliation with Israel.

> *Afterward shall the children of Israel return, and seek*
> *the Lord their God, and David their king; and shall fear*
> *the Lord and his goodness in the latter days* (Hosea 3:5).

The prophecy in Hosea 3:5 assures that the children of Israel will return, seeking the Lord their God and David their king in the latter days. This doesn't imply Israel's disappearance forever but rather a future reunion with God through Jesus, the successor of David. Jesus, the Messiah, paid the price for his people, symbolized by Hosea's redemption of his wife. The church does not replace Israel; instead, Israel is seen as the church in Revelation 19:7.

The Apostle Paul and the Spread of the Gospel:

The Apostle Paul, an Israelite, carried the message of Jesus to the Greek-speaking world, including Macedonia and Greece. This journey eventually extended west into Europe and the UK. The

Holy Spirit guided Paul's travels, following a protocol outlined in Acts 1:8: first Jerusalem, then Judea, then Samaria (Israel), and finally the ends of the earth. The idea is that Israel will play a crucial role in bringing the gospel of Jesus Christ to the farthest corners of the earth.

Adoption of Believers as Sons: God's adoption of believers as sons is emphasized in Romans 8:23 and Galatians 4:4-5.

This adoption reflects the promise that the number of the children of Israel will be as vast as the sand of the sea. Even in places where it was once said that they are not God's people, it will be declared that they are the sons of the living God.

Unity of Judah and Israel (Hosea 1:10-11)

> *Yet the number of the children of Israel shall be as the sand of the sea, which cannot be measured nor numbered; and it shall come to pass, that in the place where it was said unto them, Ye are not my people, there it shall be said unto them, <u>Ye are the sons of the living God.</u>*
>
> *Then shall the children of Judah and the children of Israel be gathered together, and appoint themselves one head, and they shall come up out of the land: for great shall be the day of Jezreel (Hosea 1:10-11).*

At this stage, Israel and Judah (the Jews) are depicted as separate entities. However, the prophecy foretells a future gathering and unity, appointing one head. This union is associated with the great day of Jezreel. Notably, Judah (the Jews) is mentioned as fighting in Jerusalem, distinct from Israel, as foretold in Zechariah 14:14. The final reconciliation of Israel and Judah is anticipated in the end times.

Lo-ruhamah

Lo-ruhamah translates to *"without compassion"* (Strongs 3819). This name signifies a critical turning point in the prophetic warnings given by the prophets. It suggests that a threshold has been reached where divine patience has run out, and the consequences of disobedience are about to unfold. Psalm 75:8 is invoked, emphasizing that the cup of divine wrath is now full and judgment is imminent.

Lo-ammi

Lo-ammi means *"for you are not my people, and I will not be your God"* (Strongs 3818). The name carries a powerful message, indicating a severance in the relationship between God and his people. The term "Ammi" means people or family, so "Lo-ammi" signifies a disowning or disconnection. This reflects a consequence of the people's actions, suggesting a moment when God withdraws His identity as their God due to their rejection and disobedience.

These names, Lo-ruhamah and Lo-ammi, collectively convey a sense of divine judgment and separation. They highlight the seriousness of the situation, where the people have strayed so far that compassion is withheld, and the relationship with God is fractured. It serves as a cautionary tale in the broader context of biblical prophecy, emphasizing the importance of remaining faithful to God's commandments to avoid reaching a point of divine judgment and estrangement.

All the Tribes of Israel

> *And Jacob called unto his sons, and said, **gather yourselves together, that I may tell you that which shall befall you <u>in the last days.</u>***

Gather yourselves together, and hear, ye sons of Jacob;
and hearken unto Israel your father.

(Genesis 49:1-2).

In Genesis 49, Jacob, also known as Israel, gathers his sons to share prophetic insights about their future. It's crucial to note that Jacob specifically mentions that he is about to reveal what will happen to them "in the last days." This is a significant detail, as it implies that the prophecies, he is about to share have relevance to a future time, not the time when he was speaking. This emphasizes the importance of paying attention to these prophecies, especially since we now live in what is considered the "last days."

Jacob's prophetic words extend to each of his sons, outlining their future paths and characteristics. Moses also provides additional insights in Deuteronomy 33. Together, these prophecies form a comprehensive view of the destiny and roles of the twelve tribes of Israel.

The significance of these prophecies is heightened in our current era. Jacob's mention of the "last days" suggests that these predictions become particularly relevant and meaningful in our time. With the advent of modern technology and the accessibility of the entire Bible, we are in a unique position to understand these prophecies better than previous generations. The increased knowledge and availability of the Old and New Testaments enable us to delve into these prophecies with more clarity and context.

The prophecies in Genesis 49 and Deuteronomy 33 outline the destinies and characteristics of each of the twelve tribes of Israel. These prophecies serve as a roadmap for understanding the roles and developments of these tribes in the unfolding of history, particularly in the last days.

By studying and reflecting on these prophecies, we gain insights into the broader narrative of God's plan for His people and the unfolding of events in the last days. It's a call to attentiveness and understanding, recognizing the relevance of ancient prophecies in our modern context.

–1–

REUBEN

Reuben in Genesis 49:3-4: Reuben, as the oldest son of Jacob, lost his inheritance due to his instability, described as being "unstable as water." This characterization stems from an incident where Reuben took the path of least resistance, displaying a lack of self-control. He committed a serious transgression by having relations with one of his father's wives. The gravity of this act is emphasized by the suggestion that he should have sought relations with his own wife, not his father's. This incident affected his standing and inheritance.

Moses' Prayer for Reuben in Deuteronomy 33:6: Despite Reuben's lapse in judgment, Moses interceded for him in prayer. Moses prayed for Reuben's life, recognizing that the act of having relations with his father's wife carried the death penalty. Instead of facing such a severe consequence, Moses blessed Reuben with many children, ensuring the continuation of his tribe.

In Numbers 2:10-16, Reuben, along with Simeon and Gad, camped on the south side, and Reuben served as their leader due to his status as the eldest. The standard of Reuben's tribe was represented by a man. This symbolism extends to heraldic emblems where men or water evoke thoughts of Reuben. For instance, in Ezekiel 1 and 10, and Revelation 4:6-8, the face of the angel is described as having the face of a man on the south side, reinforcing the association with Reuben.

These prophecies and symbolic representations highlight the complexity of Reuben's character and the interplay between his actions and the blessings and prayers invoked by Moses. Despite his shortcomings, Reuben's tribe continued through the blessing of numerous offspring, emphasizing the mercy and grace extended through intercession and divine favor. The symbolism associated with Reuben serves as a reminder of the intricate narratives woven into the biblical accounts.

File:Coat of arms of Iceland.svg - Wikipedia

Notes:

1. *Man = Israel, Reuben (camped in the South during Exodus. Deuteronomy 33:6*

2. *Man = Ephraim Zechariah 10:7*

3. *Bull = Ephraim (camped in the West during the Exodus. Deuteronomy 33:17*

4. *Eagle = Dan (camped in the North during Exodus), Numeri 2:25-31*

5. *Dragon = Dan - Genesis 49:17 17 Dan shall be a serpent by the way, an adder in the path, that biteth the horse heels, so that his rider shall fall backward. This is one very significant prophesy: the four horsemen of the Apocalypse have to come down in the end times!*

6. *Red cross = Christian cross*

7. *Blue = water = Reuben Genesis 49:4*

8. *Solid ice = water urns to ice in the cooler climates. Water = Reuben. Genesis 49:4*

9. *Staff in man's hand = authority = Judah and Israel - Genesis 49:10, Jeremiah 51:19-21*

–2–
SIMEON AND LEVI

I n Genesis 49:5-7, Simeon and Levi are addressed together as brothers with similar personalities and habits. Jacob portrays them as seemingly cruel individuals known for the instruments of cruelty they kept. He issues a strong warning about their anger and wrath, emphasizing their tendency towards fierceness and cruelty. This characterization is connected to an incident in Genesis 34:25-27 where Simeon and Levi, in response to the mistreatment of their sister Dinah, slew many men and broke down the walls of the city.

Due to their fierce actions, Jacob curses their anger and wrath, declaring that he will divide and scatter them among the tribes of Israel. This scattering is a consequence of their cruelty, and it serves as a symbolic and practical measure to prevent their unity.

Symbolism in Heraldic Emblems: Jacob's prophecy about Simeon and Levi suggests that their habits and actions will be reflected in heraldic emblems. The mention of swords and walls in their heraldic emblems is a symbolic representation of their aggressive and destructive tendencies. Those studying heraldic symbols are advised to be attentive to these elements, as they serve as reminders of the characters of Simeon and Levi.

Connection to Secret Meetings: There's a cautionary note about their secret meetings, drawing a parallel with esoteric practices like Kabbalah. The mention of secret gatherings suggests an inclination towards hidden or exclusive meetings, possibly associated with mystical or secretive knowledge.

In summary, the prophecies about Simeon and Levi in Genesis 49 highlight their fierce and cruel nature, leading to consequences of division and scattering among the tribes of Israel. The symbolism associated with swords and walls in heraldic emblems serves as a visual representation of their aggressive tendencies, and the caution about secret meetings adds an intriguing layer to their characterization.

In Deuteronomy 33, Moses outlines the significant role of the tribe of Levi. They are entrusted with the Thummim and Urim, components of the priest's breastplate. Their duties include teaching God's judgments and laws to Jacob and Israel. Additionally, they are responsible for offering incense and whole burnt sacrifices on the altar. A crucial task assigned to them is looking after the Word of God and the covenant.

Throughout history, the Levites played a vital role in preserving and teaching the law. They served as guardians of the scrolls and the sanctuary, ensuring the integrity of God's Word. During the incident of the Golden Calf, they refrained from idolatry, demonstrating their commitment to the service of the Lord. Their focus was on consecrated duties, involving teaching, administration, and the maintenance of sacred texts.

Verse 11 symbolizes the use of the sword, representing both a literal defense against adversaries and a metaphorical representation of spiritual battles. This underscores the importance of spiritual warfare and the defense of the divine principles entrusted to the Levites.

A challenge for the tribe of Levi is understanding that Jesus is the complete fulfillment of the law. The prophecy highlights the need for Jesus, who came as the sacrificial Lamb for sins. It emphasizes Jesus' future return as King, specifically from the tribe of Judah. Recognition of Jesus as the ultimate fulfillment of the law is a central theme.

In contemporary times, Levites are associated with teaching and religious administration. They traditionally rely on tithes for sustenance, supervise weights and measures, and uphold the sanctity of the scrolls.

The mention of tithing emphasizes the importance of supporting religious services and administration. Neglecting these responsibilities, as warned in the prophecy, can lead to trouble and disrupt the functioning of religious and administrative duties.

The reference to weights and measures points to potential issues with justice and fairness, as later discussed in the context of the Black Horse. The application of these principles in modern times may have deviated from their intended purpose.

In summary, the tribe of Levi played a crucial role in preserving and teaching the law, encompassing religious services and administration. The prophecy emphasizes the significance of recognizing Jesus as the fulfillment of the law, stresses the importance of tithing for sustaining religious duties, and hints at potential challenges related to justice and fairness in the modern context.

Note by author: Instead of recognizing the complete work of Jesus (Yeshua) as per the New Testament (Hebrews 10:1-18) some Levites want to re-establish the Synagogue together with animal sacrifices on the Temple Mount in Jerusalem. See **The Temple Institute - Wikipedia.** God accepted the blood of Jesus as a final offering. We can now approach God the Father directly and do not need intersession from a priest of any kind except Jesus Himself. Hebrews 10:19-22. The Third Temple will attract the attention the of the Antichrist and he will sit there. 2 Thessalonians 2:4.

Coat of arms of Bohuslän. Provincial coat of arms from the funeral of King Karl X Gustav in 1660. Available at the Royal Armoury.

Permission details

Notes:

1. *Sword = Weapons of war = Simeon and Levi Genesis 34:25-29*
2. *Tower = Simeon and Levi. They destroyed the men and the city Genesis 34:25-29.*
3. *Lion = Lord of Israel, Judah; Isaiah 5:7, Hosea 11:10.*

-3-

JUDAH

Leah, in Genesis 29:35, bore Judah and said, "Now I will praise the Lord!" Judah's name is connected with praising the Lord. From this lineage came King David, and ultimately, Jesus Christ, who is both the Lamb that was slain and the promised King of Israel and the Jews.

Due to Reuben's disqualification, as well as Simeon and Levi's disqualification, the kingship line passed to Judah, as foretold in Genesis 49:8-12. Joseph's descendants are described as having their father's children bow down before them. Joseph acted as a type of Christ. This prophetic passage points to Jesus Christ, who is referred to as a lion's whelp (son of the father). The scepter, a symbol of kingship, shall not depart from Judah. King David received the kingship, and Jesus inherited David's throne in Jerusalem. The prophecy also alludes to Jesus' riding into Jerusalem on a donkey's colt, fulfilling the prophecies of Moses and Zechariah.

The mention of washing his garments in wine and his clothes in the blood of grapes in Genesis 49:11 is seen as a reference to Jesus's second coming. This imagery is associated with a future event where Jesus goes to war against the antichrist and his forces, as described in Revelation 14:20. The blood flowing up to the horse bridles symbolizes a significant battle, and the measurement in furlongs (stadia) suggests a vast distance covered in the conflict.

Judah is symbolized as a lion, and this symbolism is expected to be reflected in heraldic emblems. Looking for lions in heraldry can be associated with the tribe of Judah. Gad and Dan also have a lion in their symbolism, and Gad is additionally represented with a crown.

The prophecies about Judah, including the recognition of Jesus as the Lion of Judah, emphasize the continuity of the kingship line and the role of Jesus as the ultimate fulfillment of these prophecies. The details about Jesus's first and second comings, as foretold in these scriptures, underscore the intricate fulfillment of prophecy in the biblical narrative.

In summary, the tribe of Judah holds a special place in biblical prophecy, being associated with praise, kingship, and the lineage of Jesus Christ. The prophecies in Genesis 49 offer a multi-layered view of Judah's significance, connecting the tribe with historical events and future fulfillments, including the second coming of Jesus. The symbolism of the lion in heraldic emblems further reinforces the unique role of Judah in the biblical narrative.

Author's Note: three tribes camped on the Eastern side in the Exodus: Judah (the leader) together with Issachar and Zebulun. Today we can still trace the people of Dutch descent to Zebulun. Their symbol was the Lion and can still be seen in the Heraldry of the Dutch and Belgium. Issachar was known to understand times and knew what to do (Chronicles 12:32) and therefore they would have known about the sun and moon and therefore times and seasons. They would have been the navigators. Like Jan van Riebeeck, the Dutch Navigator who established the Cape of Good Hope (South Africa) as a place to get fresh water and proviand for Dutch ships on their way to the East via the Cape of Good Hope. Van Riebeeck reported the first comet discovered from South Africa, the comet, later designated C/1652 Y1, was first recorded by Dutch observers at Pernambuco, Brazil on 16 December 1652.

The Bible frequently distinguishes between Israel and Judah, and this separation is evident in both the Old and New Testaments.

Johan Andreas Rautenbach

In the Old Testament, Israel and Judah represent the Northern and Southern Kingdoms, respectively. In the New Testament, the terms Jews and Gentiles (or Jews and Greeks) are used. Notably, the Greeks are considered part of Israel, often referred to as the so-called lost tribes. In the context of the Babylonian exile, Jeremia 52:29-30 records the number of Jews taken captive. This includes 832 Jews from Jerusalem in the 18th year of Nebuchadnezzar and 745 Jews from Judah in the 23rd year, totaling 4,600. The distinction between Jews and Israel is significant, as it reflects the division of the kingdom and the subsequent events.

Authors Note: Most of the Jews were taken captive to Assyria by Sennacherub, about 2/3rds. Only about a third stayed behind in Jerusalem and surrounds. Those taken to Assyria mostly got assimilated into the tribes of Israel as prophesied by Jacob in Genesis 49:7.

Sennacherub ruled from 705 BC to his own death in 681 BC

"Now in the fourteenth year of king Hezekiah did Sennacherib king of Assyria come up against all the fenced cities of Judah, and took them."
2 Kings 18:13

This is confirmed by the Sennacherub Steele. See

Sennacherib - Wikipedia

Judah, from whom the term "Jews" is derived, plays a pivotal role in biblical history. In Genesis 38, Judah takes a Canaanite wife, and through an unexpected series of events with Tamar, two sons are born: Pharez and Zarah. Pharez becomes an ancestor in the bloodline leading to Jesus Christ.

Authors note: The red hand of Ulster denotes lineage from Tamar – Zarah.
Read **Genesis 38:27-30**

Genesis 49:8-12 contains a prophecy about Judah, highlighting his lineage's importance. Due to Reuben's disqualification and Simeon and Levi's cruelty, Judah receives the kingship line. The scepter will not depart from Judah, pointing to the authority of Jesus Christ, who inherits David's throne in Jerusalem.

The prophecy in Genesis 49 symbolizes Judah as a lion, connecting to the later biblical designation of Jesus as the Lion of Judah. The imagery of Jesus washing his garments in wine and clothes in the blood of grapes alludes to his second coming, as described in Revelation 14:20.

Herod's political motivations and actions, including his marriage choices and the beheading of John the Baptist, reflect the complex dynamics of power and control in biblical times. Herod's fear of John's influence and the political landscape of that era played a role in these events.

King Solomon's disobedience led to the division of the kingdom, leaving him with only the tribe of Judah. His idolatry, influenced by foreign wives, contributed to his downfall. Solomon's straying from God's statutes and his connection to Egypt as a place to avoid showcase the consequences of disobedience.

In summary, the tribe of Judah and the term "Jews" carry significant biblical and historical weight. The distinctions between Israel and Judah, along with the complexities of political motivations and apostasy, contribute to the rich tapestry of biblical narratives. The prophecies concerning Judah's lineage, especially in Genesis 49, foreshadow the coming of Jesus Christ, the Lion of Judah, and His role as the ultimate authority.

Instructions to the Kings of Israel

*But he shall not **multiply horses to himself**, nor cause the people to **return to Egypt,** to the end that he should multiply horses: forasmuch as the Lord hath said unto you, Ye shall henceforth return no more that way.*

*17 Neither shall he **multiply wives to himself**, that his heart turn not away: neither shall he greatly **multiply to himself silver and gold.***

*18 And it shall be, when he sitteth upon the throne of his kingdom, that he shall **write him a copy of this law in a book** out of that which is before the priests the Levites:*

*¹⁹And it shall be with him, and he shall read therein all the days of his life: that he **may learn to fear the** LORD **his God,** to keep all the words of this law and these statutes, to do them:*

That his heart be not lifted up above his brethren, and that he turns not aside from the commandment, to the right hand, or to the left: to the end that he may prolong his days in his kingdom, he, and his children, in the midst of Israel. **Deuteronomy 17:18-20**

Do not multiply horses: The king should not amass a large number of horses for himself, especially by returning to Egypt for more.

Do not return to Egypt: The king is explicitly instructed not to lead the people back to Egypt, emphasizing a commitment to move forward and not rely on Egypt's resources.

Do not multiply wives: The king should refrain from having an excessive number of wives, preventing his heart from turning away from the Lord.

Do not multiply silver and gold: Accumulating vast wealth in silver and gold is discouraged, reminding the king not to prioritize material wealth.

Write a copy of the Law: The king is to personally write a copy of the law from what is before the priests, emphasizing a direct engagement with God's commands.

Learn to fear the Lord: Reading the law daily is aimed at cultivating a genuine fear of the Lord, ensuring obedience to His words and statutes.

Lesson from Solomon: Solomon, despite being one of the wisest kings, disobeyed these specific instructions. He multiplied horses, returned to Egypt, had numerous wives, amassed great wealth, and, ultimately, turned away from the Lord by bowing down to foreign gods. Solomon's actions serve as a cautionary tale, demonstrating the consequences of disobedience to God's explicit commands.

These instructions are not generic; they were tailored for the kings of Israel, like King Solomon. The principles, however, offer timeless wisdom. They caution against the allure of materialism, reliance on foreign powers, and the importance of prioritizing a relationship with God over worldly pursuits. In a contemporary context, the warnings about accumulating wealth and the potential misuse of technology (symbolized by 666) resonate, urging individuals to stay grounded in faith and avoid succumbing to worldly temptations. Ye cannot serve God and mammon. Luke 16:13

The exploration of Egyptian mythology reveals a pantheon of gods and goddesses, each with distinct attributes and significance (10 Egyptian Gods and Goddesses - hence the 10 plagues). Notably, the worship of Isis and Horus, a mother and son duo, has persisted throughout history, evolving into the contemporary veneration of the "Queen of Heaven." This continuity in worship reflects the enduring nature of certain religious practices.

The roots of mother and child worship extend to Babylon, where Nimrod, described as a rebel and potentially identified with Gilgamesh, played a pivotal role (Genesis 10:10). Nimrod's association with tyranny and rebellion, as noted by Josephus in Antiquities of the Jews, underscores the historical and symbolic significance attached to his figure (Josephus - Ant. I: iv: 2).

The construction of the Tower of Babel is contextualized as a portal to the demonic world, mirroring contemporary concerns about initiatives like CERN and their exploration of alternate dimensions (Genesis 11:6). The suggestion that Babylon was built to withstand a flood is disputed, with a focus on the potential goal of resurrecting demons eradicated during the biblical flood.

The interpretation of locusts in the biblical context, particularly in Revelation, introduces symbolic layers. While locusts resembling horses with faces like men are considered as possible metaphors for pilots of helicopters, those emerging from the bottomless pit are unequivocally associated with demons (Revelation 9:7, Revelation 9:1-3). The symbolic nature of locusts as representations of demons is emphasized in various biblical references, including Malachi 3:11 and Revelation 9:1-3.

Within this framework, there exists a speculative notion of an ongoing plan to resurrect demons, aligning with biblical narratives (Genesis 11:6). This perspective is intertwined with cautionary biblical admonitions against relying on human imaginations and underscores the idea that the adversary, Satan, is a persistent force aiming to deceive and wreak havoc (2 Corinthians 10:5, Ezekiel 28:18).

The Bottomless Pit

The inner core of the Earth, a dense sphere composed mostly of iron, presents extreme conditions with a radius of approximately

1,220 kilometers (758 miles). This intensely hot region boasts temperatures soaring to about 5,200° Celsius (9,392° Fahrenheit) and is subjected to a staggering pressure of nearly 3.6 million atmospheres (atm). Despite the intense heat, the inner core does not exist in a molten or liquid state, primarily due to the extreme pressure and density that confines iron atoms, making them unable to move freely. The inner core, instead, exhibits properties akin to a solid, perhaps described as a type of plasma that behaves with solidity.

Drawing a metaphorical connection to the inner core, the narrative shifts to historical figures, namely Nimrod, or Ninus, and his wife Semiramis. According to legend, Semiramis ascended to become the queen of Assyria and Babylon. Notably, she played a significant role in the restoration of ancient Babylon, overseeing the construction of a formidable brick wall that encircled the entire city. A peculiar twist in the legend suggests that she married her son, initiating the narrative of mother-son worship (Wikipedia - Semiramis).

This historical account resonates with the concept of mother-and-child worship, echoing the enduring presence of such beliefs in contemporary religious practices. The mention of a high brick wall around the city in connection to the legend draws attention to symbolic elements, prompting consideration of passages like Daniel 11:38, which mentions the "god of forces."

The narrative concludes by pointing out the persistence of mother-and-child worship, coupled with the veneration of the Queen of Heaven and the worship of deceased saints. It draws parallels between these practices and the act of praying to forefather spirits, highlighting the possible influence of familiar spirits, as seen in 1 Samuel 28. The assertion emphasizes the incontrovertible evidence of Jesus overcoming death and reigning in heaven, extending His authority to His witnesses on Earth, as indicated in Hosea 6:3. The exploration invites contemplation on the endurance of certain religious motifs throughout history.

Notes:

1. *The young lions and the old lion represent Judah. Genesis 49:8-12.*
2. *Jesus is The Lion of Judah: Revelation 5:5*
3. *Jesus is the Root of David. Revelation 5:5*
4. *Judah refers to praise and worship and King David played the harp. 1 Samuel 16:23.*
5. *The three lions could represent England, Scotland and Wales and the Harp would represent Ireland. I do not want to be dogmatic here. Moses and Israel (Jacob) were explicitly talking about symbols of the end times.*

-4-

ZEBULUN

Leah's exclamation in Genesis 30:20 upon bearing her sixth son, whom she named Zebulun, reflects a sense of honor and elevation. The name Zebulun is derived from the Hebrew word "Zevul," signifying an exalted house or a dwelling associated with honor. Leah perceived this birth as a source of honor and a manifestation of God's favor, attributing her elevated status to the birth of six sons, an event she believed would draw her husband Jacob to dwell with her.

The biblical account, supported by Strong's Concordance (2073 zebul), underscores the theme of elevation and lofty abode associated with Zebulun. Spiritually, the tribe of Zebulun was characterized by high moral values. Geographically, their dwelling was situated at sea level, and to this day, a part of their region remains slightly below sea level. The impact of Leah's genes on half of the Israelite tribes reflects her significant contribution to the overall gene pool.

The prophecy in Genesis 49:13 further illuminates Zebulun's connection to maritime activities. Zebulun was destined to dwell at the haven of the sea, becoming a haven for ships. Their border extended to Zidon, a location where they likely acquired their expertise in shipbuilding and navigation. In biblical times, the tribe of Zebulun engaged in fishing, and when Jesus visited their region, many were fishermen, establishing a historical connection to their maritime legacy.

During the 1600-1700s, Zebulun, represented by the Dutch people, experienced a period of economic prosperity through the Dutch East India Company (VOC). This company played a pivotal role in trade with Asia, sending numerous Europeans to work in Asia trade on thousands of ships. The Dutch, with Rotterdam and Antwerp ranking as the top two container ports in Europe, continue to be significant players in maritime trade.

The historical navigation of Jan van Riebeeck around the Cape of Good Hope in 1652 marked the Dutch presence in South Africa. Van Riebeeck, a navigator, also recorded a comet in 1652, commemorated by a vow and covenant made by the Afrikaners on 6 April 1654. Hudson, appointed by the Dutch to find an Eastward trade route, instead explored the Upper New York Bay on 11 September 1609. Centuries later, on 11 September 2001, the ship Half Moon, symbolically retracing Hudson's route, witnessed the tragic events of the Twin Towers' destruction. The celestial alignment with the moon during this period serves as a striking historical marker.

Coat of arms of William I as "sovereign prince", 1813–1815

Unknown author - Wapenregister van de Nederlandse adel Hoge Raad van Adel 1814 - 2014 Auteur: Coen O.A. Schimmelpenninck van der Oije, Egbert Wolleswinkel, Jos van den Borne, Conrad Gietman Uitgave: WBooks, 2014 p.127

Soevereine_vorst_der_Verenigde_Nederlanden_wapen 1814-1815

Soevereine vorst der Verenigde Nederlanden wapen - Coat of arms of the Netherlands - Wikipedia

Note by Author: *This book by Schimmelpenninck is in the Public Domain:*

Notes:

1. *The lion with coronet denotes a kingdom. Revelation 1:6 and 5:10, Gen 49:10-11*
2. *The lion was the symbol of Judah. Issachar and Zebulun camped with Judah on the Eastern side during the Exodus from Egypt. Numbers 2:1-9*
3. *The Dutch are mainly descended from Zebulun.*
4. *The sword is a symbol of Israel: Jeremia 51:19-21.*
5. *Je Maintiendrai* = French for "I shall maintain". *Job 13:15*
6. *Bundle of arrows = Israel – Numbers 24:8 God brought him forth out of Egypt; he hath as it were the strength of a unicorn: he shall eat up the nations his enemies, and shall break their bones, and pierce them through with his arrows.*

–5–

ISSACHAR

Genesis 49:14-15 provides intriguing insights into the character and role of Issachar. Depicted as a robust donkey lying down between two burdens or sheepfolds (mishpethayim), Issachar emerges as a hardworking and sturdy individual. The imagery suggests not only diligence and strength but also a peaceful and neutral disposition, drawing comparisons to a people known for their amiable nature, much like the Swiss.

The name Issachar, derived from Strong's Concordance (3485 Yissaskar), carries the meaning "there is recompense." This concept of recompense may symbolize Issachar's industriousness, implying that their hard work brings forth rewards or benefits.

1 Chronicles 12:32 sheds light on Issachar's distinctive role among the tribes, noting that the children of Issachar possessed an understanding of the times, guiding Israel in their actions. This specialized knowledge points to an aptitude for celestial observation and navigation, positioning Issachar as navigators for sea-faring tribes like Dan, Naphtali, Zebulun, and Asher.

Deuteronomy 33:18 reaffirms the close association between Issachar and Zebulun, highlighting Zebulun's ventures outside, while Issachar remains in their tents. This arrangement suggests that Issachar played a crucial role in providing navigational expertise, particularly considering Zebulun's maritime activities.

In the camp setup outlined in Numbers 2:3-9, Judah, Issachar, and Zebulun consistently formed a close-knit grouping in the East. This cohesive arrangement implies a strong bond and shared responsibilities among these tribes.

The phrase "understanding the times" in 1 Chronicles 12:32 implies a grasp of celestial or chronological knowledge. This mastery might extend to clockwork precision, evoking parallels with the renowned Swiss watches celebrated for their accuracy and craftsmanship. The Swiss watchmaking tradition, synonymous with precision and reliability, resonates with Issachar's purported expertise.

Yair Davidiy's assertion that a remnant of Issachar can be found in Switzerland and Finland aligns with the idea that Issachar's descendants may have played a role in shaping the cultures of these regions. The metaphor of the loaded donkey in Genesis 49:14-15 symbolizes the prosperity and contributions of Issachar, analogous to the bounty carried by a burdened yet strong donkey.

Personal command-sign of the King of Sweden - Coat of arms of Sweden - Wikipedia Adopted 1448 – 17 November 1905. This emblem is in the Public Domain

Permission details

<u>Great coat of arms of Sweden (shield) - Coat of arms of Sweden - Wikipedia</u>

Notes:

1. *Crowns = kingdom, Judah, Gad - Gen 49:10-11*
2. *Lion = Israel, Judah, Dan. Gad - Gen 49:9*
3. *Eagle = Dan - Numbers 2:25-31*
4. *Stars = Israel, Issachar: Genesis 26:4-5, 1 Chron 12:32 (Men that had understanding of the times).*
5. *Water = Reuben – Genesis 49:4*
6. *Towers = Simeon, Levi – Genesis 49:6*
7. *JAR = Asher – Genesis 49:20*

–6–

DAN

Genesis 49:16-18

*Dan shall **judge** his people, as one of the tribes of Israel.*
*Dan shall be a **serpent** by the way, an adder in the **path**,*
*that biteth the horse heels, so that his **rider shall fall***
backward.
*I have waited for thy **salvation, O Lord.***

G enesis 49:16-18 provides a distinctive glimpse into the
character and destiny of the tribe of Dan. The name
Dan, as per Strong's Concordance 1835, translates to
"judge," indicating a leadership role within Israel. This association
is reflected in the historical figure of Samson, a renowned leader
from the tribe of Dan, as chronicled in Judges 13.

*Author's Note: **Samson's** role in Israel has been underplayed in
commentaries throughout history. But let us look at the facts: he
singlehandedly wiped out the whole leadership of the King and his whole
government, the leadership of the Military as well as the Religious top
structure. This weakened the Philistines to a point where the later kings
of Israel like Saul, David and Salomon could subdue the whole area of the
Philistines with the help of the Pharao of Egypt who conquered a region
and gave a city as a gift for his Egyptian bride. 1 Kings 9:16, 1 Kings 3:1.*

The tribe of Dan could not conquer the Philistines because they had 30000 chariots and 6000 horsemen as well as thousands of infantry on the low-lying ground. 1 Samuel 13:5-14. They were the last tribe to get real estate and nobody seemed to help them conquer the area. They had to move North to a place they called Dan in the North. Samson's job was to start weakening the Philistines and this he did. Judges 13:4-5. Samson took down 5 Philistine leaders and 3000 people, mostly leaders. Judges 16:29-31. This happened in Gaza. Judges 16:21. There is still trouble in Gaza today – with the Philistines or is it Palestinians under Hamas. See Strongs 2555 = chamas: חָמָס = violence, wrong.

Deuteronomy 33:22 describes Dan as a lion's whelp leaping from Bashan. In contemporary geography, Bashan predominantly falls within the borders of Syria. In ancient times, Bashan was inhabited by Og, the giant king, identified as a Nephilim—a hybrid of fallen angels and human women. Deuteronomy 3:11 attests to Og's extraordinary stature, noting his iron bed measuring 9 by 4 cubits (13.5 feet). This suggests the potential encounters of Dan and his descendants with giants, or Nephilim. Strongs 5303: נְפִיל = nephilim: "giants".

Genesis 49:17 prophesies that Dan will confront horsemen on war horses, potentially symbolizing spiritual battles. The reference to horses aligns with imagery found in Revelation 6 and Zechariah 6, where various colored horses with riders represent spiritual forces. This encounter may involve Dan, represented as an eagle, along with Ephraim and Manasseh, symbolized as arrows and branches, and the rest of the tribes.

The intriguing statement in verse 18, "I have waited for thy salvation, O Lord," implies a patient anticipation for the salvation brought by the Lord Himself. This aligns with the fundamental Christian belief that Jesus Christ is the embodiment of salvation, as emphasized in Romans 10:9 and Acts 4:12. Dan, symbolized as the judge, appears to await the ultimate salvation offered by Jesus Christ.

Jeremiah 50:23 and 51:19-21 unveil profound spiritual imagery, emphasizing the breaking of bonds and the divine role of Israel as God's instrument in a spiritual battle. In Jeremiah 50:23, the metaphorical hammer of the entire earth is cut asunder and broken, symbolizing the collapse of Babylon as a desolation among the nations. It is crucial to note that Babylon is depicted as a spiritual place, and even Jesus was crucified there, highlighting its symbolic significance. Revelation 11:8. This place is also referred to as Sodom and Egypt.

Jeremiah 51:19-21 further elaborates on Israel's unique position as the battle axe and weapons of war in the hands of God.

Jeremiah 51:19-21

The portion of Jacob is not like them; for he is the former of all things: and Israel is the rod of his inheritance: the Lord of hosts is his name.

Thou art my <u>battle axe</u> and weapons of war: for with thee will I break in pieces the nations, and with thee will I destroy kingdoms;

And with thee will I break in pieces the horse and his rider; and with thee will I break in pieces the chariot and his rider;

The passage emphasizes the distinction of Jacob, the former of all things, and Israel, the rod of God's inheritance. The Lord of hosts claims Israel as His battle axe and declares His intention to break nations and destroy kingdoms through them.

Authors note: The battle axe was the Gothic (Gad's) weapon of choice and left its mark on the dead. Often the head and shoulder were severed. See Ancient Irish Weapons: The Battle-axe (libraryireland.com)

Then there are 4 demonic riders waiting on the white, the red, the black and the green horse to take down at the end! It is a given, it will happen.

The spiritual nature of the battle is underscored as God declares, "with thee will I break in pieces **the horse and his rider.**" This imagery echoes a spiritual warfare scenario, where Israel, representing the 2 witnesses, the church, and all the tribes, is fully armed and prepared for battle against the false prophet, the antichrist, and the forces symbolized by the four horsemen of the Apocalypse. Ezekiel 37 portrays the army of the Lord, emphasizing the unity of the whole house of Israel, encompassing all the tribes, not solely the Jews of Judah.

In essence, these passages foreshadow a spiritual battle wherein Israel, equipped and empowered by God, plays a pivotal role in breaking the bonds and defeating the spiritual adversaries that oppose the divine purpose. The imagery aligns with the overarching narrative of a spiritual struggle, transcending mere earthly conflicts.

Ezekiel 37:16 unveils a symbolic prophecy, instructing the son of man to take two sticks and inscribe them, one for Judah and the children of Israel, and the other for Joseph, specifically noting the stick of Ephraim and all the house of Israel his companions.

Ezekiel 37:16

*Moreover, thou son of man, take thee one stick, and write upon it, **For Judah, and for the children of Israel his companions:** then take another stick, and write upon it, **For Joseph, the stick of Ephraim and for all the house of Israel his companions:***

This division between Judah and Israel (representing the Northern Kingdom) has been a recurring theme, highlighting their distinct identities.

The significance of Ephraim, representing Joseph and all the tribes of Israel, becomes particularly noteworthy. The symbolism of the sticks serves as a powerful metaphor, signifying the unity and coming together of these divided entities. Interestingly, there are 13 sticks in total, considering Ephraim and Manasseh separately.

A striking parallel is drawn to the imagery found in the national symbol of the United States—the claws of the eagle. The eagle, a prominent symbol in American iconography, carries the idea of unity, strength, and a connection to ancient Israel. In this context, the 13 sticks can be seen as representative of the 13 original colonies and, in a broader sense, the diverse groups that make up the American nation.

The imagery echoes Ezekiel's vision of the reunification of Israel and Judah, pointing towards a symbolic representation in the historical and cultural fabric of the United States. The inclusion of Ephraim and Manasseh in the sticks signifies a broader unity encompassing all the tribes. This interpretation aligns with the idea that certain aspects of the nation's identity and destiny may carry echoes of the ancient biblical narrative.

In the intricate symbolism of the Great Seal, the foresight of God is perceived, with echoes of Israel's ancient tribes embedded within. Genesis 49:22-23, conveying Jacob's perspective on the fruitful bough and the archers, unfolds layers of meaning in this enigmatic design. The eagle, emblematic of Dan, emerges as a leader among the northern tribes, while the stars allude to Joseph's dream, symbolizing the uncountable descendants promised to Abraham—like the stars of the heavens.

Dan, from the onset, was a seafaring nation, acquiring nautical skills from their Phoenician neighbors, Tyrus and Sidon. With a town named Dan after their patriarch, formerly Laish, they embraced shipbuilding and sailing, as evidenced in Judges 18:29. Stretching "from Dan to Beersheba," the realm of Dan encompassed the northern expanse, and the tribe's association with the sea is palpable in its enduring maritime legacy.

Intriguingly, the description in 2 Samuel 17:11, portraying Israel as countless as the sand of the sea, aligns with Dan's distinctiveness, contrasting with the enumerable Jews of Judah. Judges 5:17 underscores Dan's maritime pursuits, dwelling on their ships while Gilead, akin to the Gaul's, resided beyond the Jordan, known today as Jordania within Israel's territory.

The skilled craftsmanship of the tribe of Dan is further highlighted. Aholiab, from the tribe of Dan, was endowed with wisdom for woodwork and fabric arts. As an engraver and master of materials necessary for shipbuilding, his contribution is immortalized in Exodus 31:6 and 1 Kings 7:14. Naphtali, a full brother of Dan, is also mentioned in the latter reference, emphasizing the collaborative prowess of these sibling tribes.

Thus, within the folds of the Great Seal, the multifaceted tapestry of Israel's history and tribes unfolds, offering a glimpse into the intricate design inspired by ancient biblical narratives.

Denmark, etymologically linked to the tribe of Dan, stands as a testament to the historical and cultural connections with this ancient tribe. According to Yair Davidiy in "The Tribes" (page 179 and beyond), Denmark's nomenclature finds its roots in the tribe of Dan, and a significant population of Danes can trace their heritage back to this tribe. Hushim, the son of Dan, is mentioned in Genesis 46:23, although Dan is recognized as the second-largest tribe, likely having more sons, even if unspecified.

Dan's influence extends beyond Denmark, resonating among the Celts and leaving intriguing linguistic imprints. Noteworthy names such as Dangalae, meaning Dan of Galilee, and Damnae, akin to Damnoni of Scotland, exemplify the far-reaching impact of Dan's legacy. Dannonia, applied to Devon and Cornwall in Southwest England, pays homage to the tribe of Dan. The Welsh legend of the children of Don adds another layer to this intricate tapestry.

Geographic names also bear the imprint of Dan, exemplified by the Danube River, known as Celtic Danu or Don. The rivers Danube, Dnieper, and Dniester, along with numerous places in the UK featuring Danu or Don, reflect the enduring influence of the tribe of Dan. Variations such as Danubius or Danuvius in Latin and Dunarea or Donaris in Romanian underscore the linguistic transformations while preserving the essence of the original name.

The historical expertise of the tribe of Dan in metalworking, particularly shipbuilding, finds echoes in Aholiab (Exodus 31:6) and Hiram (2 Chronicles 2:3-14), both renowned as expert artisans and metalworkers. This legacy persists to the present day, with the Danes maintaining a prominent position in the global containership industry. The private enterprise of Danish shipbuilders, exemplified by their colossal and technologically advanced ships, attests to the enduring skills and legacy of the tribe of Dan.

Maersk, a global giant in container shipping and vessel operation, held the distinction of being the largest in its industry from 1996 until 2021. Headquartered in Copenhagen, Denmark, Maersk has been a prominent player in maritime trade and shipping. The company's influence extends to the construction of massive containerships and offshore rigs, emphasizing Denmark's enduring role in the maritime sector.

Despite the evolving dynamics of the shipping industry, Maersk remains at the forefront of innovation. The company continues to build colossal containerships, contributing to its legacy as a major player in global shipping and vessel operations. Notably, Maersk has adopted sustainable practices, as demonstrated by its utilization of carbon-neutral methanol to fuel containers, aligning with contemporary environmental concerns.

In considering the broader context of the tribes of Israel, it becomes evident that these ancient tribes have not vanished but have left indelible imprints on the present. Through careful study, their legacies can be traced to various regions, and Denmark, associated with the tribe of Dan, exemplifies this continuity. The influence of Dan, known for its maritime expertise, is vividly reflected in Denmark's prominent position in the global shipping industry, with companies like Maersk leading the way.

Johan Andreas Rautenbach

It is crucial to dispel misconceptions about the tribes of Israel disappearing, as their descendants and cultural influences persist across time and geography. The narrative propagated by Satan, suggesting God's rejection of His people, stands debunked through the ongoing presence and impact of these tribes. The distinction between Jews and Israelites is vital. Also, the word Semites, which means descendants of Shem, the forebear of Abram (Genesis 11:10-32) encompasses a diverse range of nations, including Arabs, Indians, and various European groups. Shem was still alive when Abram was born. The tribes, dispersed but not forgotten, continue to play roles in shaping the modern world.

While supporting Israel and its people is commendable, it is essential to approach such matters with discernment and seek guidance from the Holy Spirit. Proverbs 3:5-6 underscores the importance of trusting in the Lord, acknowledging Him in all endeavors, and relying on His direction. The complexity of situations and the uncertainty of the future highlight the need for a reliance on divine wisdom rather than solely leaning on human understanding. Therefore, careful consideration and seeking divine guidance are imperative in navigating the intricacies of supporting various causes.

Achievement
File:Greater coat of arms of the United States.svg - Wikimedia Commons

Notes:

1. *Eagle: Strongs 5404 Nesher: Firstly, the symbol belongs to God Exodus 19:4, Psalm 91:1-4*
2. *Eagle – secondly belongs to the face of an Angel that protects Israel and stand before God: Ezekiel 1:10, Revelation 4:7*
3. *Eagle – thirdly the symbol belongs to the tribe of Dan who camped on the North side during the Exodus. Numbers 2:25. The angel had a face of an Eagle on the North side. Revelation 4:7.*
4. *Eagle – fourthly the symbol belongs to the USA. Now my contention is that all the tribes of Israel can be found in the USA.*
5. *13 Stars = Jacob (Israel) had 12 sons. Genesis 49. But he adopted the 2 sons of Joseph (Genesis 48:5) who now represent Joseph. Manasseh and Ephraim take the place of Joseph. Ezekiel 37:19. The stars are the children of Jacob. Genesis 37:9. Also Abraham and Isaac and Jacob had God's word that his offspring would be like the stars of heaven and the whole world will be blessed by them. Genesis 26:4*
6. *The bough with fruit and arrows is the symbols of Joseph = Ephraim and Manasseh. Genesis 49:22. Sword and bow are symbols of Israel. Genesis 48:22. Ephraim would become many nations and would be bigger than Manasse the eldest. Therefore.*

I contend that Ephraim would be the USA and Manasse the UK. Genesis 49:19.

7. *The other side of the Great Seal I will discuss elsewhere. Suffice it to say it is full of occultic symbols from Egypt which God told King Solomon to stay away from. He did not and disobeyed God's explicit instructions. 1 Kings 11:4. This resulted in his following the occult into the occultic 666. 1 Kings 10:14. You cannot serve God and Mammon. One will lose out.*

–7–

GAD

The biblical narrative unfolds intriguingly as it casts light on the tribe of Gad. Leah, in her proclamation of good fortune, names her son Gad, symbolizing the blessings associated with this tribe. In the course of prophecy, Jacob envisions a troop coming against Gad, yet he foretells that Gad will ultimately overcome. This prophecy takes on a distinctive resonance in the context of Great Britain, particularly during its historical zenith marked by expansive military endeavors and imperial glory.

The Hebrew term "gedud" (Strongs 1416), signifying a troop or band, resonates with the martial prowess historically exhibited by Great Britain. The British Isles, comprising various tribes such as the English, Scottish, Irish, and Welsh, witnessed a multitude of invasions and conquests over the years. The prophetic parallels between Gad enlarging, dwelling as a lion, and tearing the arm with a crown find an uncanny echo in the historical narrative of Great Britain's imperial dominion.

Moses, in his prophetic blessing over Gad, further underscores the imagery of a lion and a kingdom. The lion, symbolic of strength and majesty, aligns with the historical might of the British Empire. The tearing of the arm, connoting victory over adversaries, takes on significance when viewed through the lens of Britain's triumphs in warfare and global influence.

Authors note: see note on Battle Axe above. Ancient Irish Weapons: The Battle-axe (libraryireland.com)

Gad's resemblance to the Hebrew word for Goth, along with the identification of the northern tribes in Scandinavia, adds a layer of complexity to the geographic dispersal of these tribes. The historical invasions from the North, possibly connecting to Scandinavia, and the influx from the East, including Anglo-Saxons and Goths, contribute to the multifaceted tapestry of Israelite tribes in the British Isles.

In essence, the convergence of fortune, troops, lions, and crowns presents a compelling case for identifying Gad's descendants with the historical trajectory of Great Britain. The intricate interplay of biblical prophecy and historical events serves as a testament to the enduring nature of God's promises and the unfolding of divine providence.

Examining the Royal Arms of Great Britain from 1714 to 1800 through a biblical lens offers a fascinating perspective, unveiling symbolic elements tied to various Israelite tribes.

The presence of crowns in the Royal Arms aligns with the biblical tribes of Gad and Judah. The crown, symbolizing royalty and authority, resonates with the historical narrative of these tribes. The biblical prophecies regarding Gad's triumph and Judah's enduring royal lineage find a symbolic expression in the regal crowns.

Lions, a recurrent symbol in the heraldry, represent the biblical tribes of Judah, Dan, and Gad. The lion, emblematic of strength and courage, aligns with the prophecy of Jacob in Genesis 49, where Judah is referred to as a lion's cub. The inclusion of lions in the Royal Arms reflects a connection to these significant tribes.

The depiction of a unicorn in the Royal Arms takes us back to Moses' prophecy in Deuteronomy 33:17. The unicorn, described as having horns like the firstling of a bullock, symbolizes Ephraim and Manasseh. Moses, as a prophet, conveyed the divine message, affirming the unique heraldic emblem associated with these tribes. The unicorn, pushing people to the ends of the earth, mirrors the dispersal and influence of Ephraim and Manasseh.

The choice of a unicorn as a heraldic symbol is distinctive, and its alignment with the biblical narrative adds a layer of significance. The acknowledgment of Ephraim and Manasseh, and by extension, all of Israel, reinforces the intertwining of historical symbols and divine promises.

In essence, the Royal Arms of Great Britain, with its crowns, lions, and unicorn, serves as a visual tapestry connecting the nation's heraldic heritage to the biblical prophecies and the enduring legacy of the Israelite tribes.

Author's Note: Deuteronomy 33:17 talks about the horns of a bull (Strongs 7794: Shor = a head of cattle (bullock, ox, etc.) and a unicorn, which means one horn and is translated from Strongs 7214: reem as a wild ox. That is a misunderstanding in my opinion. The animal has one horn. It is also represented as a horse with one horn, that makes it a mythical animal. Maybe an extinct animal or maybe a rhinoceros. The point is you will find the unicorn as a national symbol only in the UK. Period.

Numbers 23:19-24

God is not a man, that he should lie; *neither the son of man, that he should repent: hath he said, and shall he not do it? or hath he spoken, and shall he not make it good?*

*Behold, **I have received commandment to bless:** and he hath blessed; and I cannot reverse it.*

*He hath not beheld iniquity in Jacob, neither hath he seen perverseness in Israel: The Lord his God is with him, **and the shout of a king is among them.***

God brought them out of Egypt; he hath as it were the
strength of a unicorn. (Strongs 7214. Reem = רְאֵם)

Surely there is no enchantment against Jacob, neither
is there any divination against Israel: according to this
time it shall be said of Jacob and of Israel, What hath
God wrought!

Behold, the people shall rise up as a great lion, and
lift up himself as a young lion: *he shall not lie down*
until he eat of the prey, and drink the blood of the slain.

Examining the heraldic emblems in light of Numbers 23:19-24
and the biblical narrative provides insights into the symbolism of
the United Kingdom, reflecting the divine promises made to the
Israelite tribes.

Crown, Horn of a Unicorn, Great Lion, and Young Lion: The
biblical passage in Numbers underscores the unity of all the tribes
of Israel, and the symbols of a crown, horn of a unicorn, great lion,
and young lion in the heraldry of the United Kingdom resonate
with this collective identity. The divine promises given to Israel
find symbolic representation in these emblems, signifying strength,
kingship, and the unity of the nation.

The harp as a symbol represents the biblical King David,
known for his musical talents. It aligns with the rich heritage of
the Davidic line, emphasizing the enduring legacy of King David
within the nation's history.

The Fleur de Lis and Roses carry biblical significance,
representing the "Lily of the valleys" (Song of Solomon 2:1),
emphasizing purity and beauty. This symbolism is reinforced by
biblical references in Matthew 6:28-29 and Hosea 14:5, connecting
the emblems to spiritual and scriptural themes.

The horse, a symbol associated with the troop of Gad and Dan
(Genesis 49:17), adds a biblical layer to the heraldic emblems. This

reinforces the connection between the symbols and the historical journey of the Israelite tribes.

"Dieu et Mon Droit" and "Honi soit qui mal y pense": The motto "Dieu et Mon Droit" (My God and my right hand) is linked to the sword, symbolizing Gad (Genesis 49:19) and Simeon and Levi (Genesis 49:5-7). The motto "Honi soit qui mal y pense" (Shame on anyone who thinks evil of it) reflects resilience against those who question the legitimacy and righteousness of the symbols.

The heraldic emblems, therefore, serve as a visual tapestry, weaving together biblical promises, historical narratives, and national identity. They bear witness to the enduring connection between the United Kingdom and the biblical heritage of the Israelite tribes.

The Bible tells us that the tribe of Gad was exiled with Reuben and the half tribe of Manasseh to Halah, Habor, the river of and to Harah 1 Cron 5:26. Gad (Goth) reappeared as the Guti. From there they moved west in Europe and Scandinavia where they can still be identified as a group in Sweden.

The historical connection between Swedish men enlisting in the Byzantine Varangian Guard and the biblical tribe of Gad is intriguing, especially considering the choice of weaponry and the mention of tearing the arm with the crown of the head in Deuteronomy 33:20.

The enlistment of Swedish men in the Byzantine Varangian Guard, coupled with the term "Greece" being used to describe the Byzantine Empire, draws an interesting parallel with the term "Greeks" in the New Testament. The New Testament addresses Israelites who were often referred to as Greeks, and the fact that the Varangian Guard served in the Byzantine Empire, a region that became synonymous with the term "Greece," adds a historical layer to this biblical connection.

The unique fighting style of the Goths, characterized by the use of battle axes to cut off the enemy's head and one shoulder with a single blow, aligns with the description in Deuteronomy 33:20

regarding Gad. The biblical verse speaks of Gad dwelling as a lion and tearing the arm with the crown of the head. The battle axe, an effective and symbolic weapon, becomes a tangible expression of the blessings upon Gad.

Deuteronomy 33:20 reads: *"Blessed be he that enlargeth Gad: he dwelleth as a lion, and teareth the arm with the crown of the head."* The tearing of the arm with the crown of the head can be seen metaphorically in the prowess of the Gothic warriors using battle axes, emphasizing Gad's strength and military success.

In essence, the historical migration of Swedish men to the Byzantine Varangian Guard not only reflects the geopolitical dynamics of the time but also echoes biblical themes associated with the tribe of Gad. The use of battle axes, reminiscent of Gad's tearing of the arm, adds a fascinating dimension to the historical connection between Old Testament prophecies and the actions of specific tribes and nations.

The historical context of the separation of Sweden and Denmark-Norway, particularly the delineation of borders and the mention of the Westrogothic Law, offers an intriguing link to biblical tribes, especially Naphtali and Gad.

Separation of Sweden and Denmark-Norway (1523-1658): The separation of Sweden and Denmark-Norway in 1523, following the breakup of the Kalmar Union, signifies a significant shift in geopolitical dynamics. The subsequent delineation of borders, especially the mention of provinces like Scania, Blekinge, Bohuslän, and Halland, adds depth to the historical narrative.

The reference to Norway as the region where Naphtali settled draws a biblical connection. Naphtali, being a full brother of Dan, is one of the tribes of Israel. Exploring the geographical links between Norway and Naphtali enhances the understanding of historical migrations and settlements of these biblical tribes.

The mention of the Westrogothic Law and its association with the Goths is noteworthy. The term "Goth" is etymologically linked to Gad, one of the tribes of Israel. The presence of Goths in Sweden aligns with the biblical narrative, especially considering Gad's role as a warrior tribe.

The historical events, including the Treaty of Roskilde in 1645, contribute to the establishment of the Denmark-Sweden border along the Øresund. The reference to six border marks in the 11th century, possibly linked to the known border until 1645, adds a layer of historical continuity.

In summary, the historical separation of Sweden and Denmark-Norway, the connection of Norway to Naphtali, and the mention of the Westrogothic Law allude to a rich historical tapestry that intersects with biblical narratives, specifically related to the tribes of Naphtali and Gad.

Royal Coat of Arms of the United Kingdom (Tudor crown) - Coat of arms of the United Kingdom - Wikipedia. Adopted 1837.

Notes:

1. *The Lion represent Israel, Judah, Gad, Dan. Numbers 23:19-24 and scriptures mentioned above. Jesus is called The Lion of Judah. Revelation 5:5*

2. *The crown represents a kingdom. Genesis 49:10.*

3. *The unicorn represents Israel. Numbers 34:8. Strongs 7214 reem = ראם.* **God brought them out of Egypt; he hath as it were the strength of an unicorn. Numbers 24:8**

4. *The horse represents Dan:* **Genesis 49:17**

5. *Ephraim and Manasseh = Bull and Unicorn, Deuteronomy 33:17. His glory is like the firstling of his bullock, and his horns are like the horns of unicorns: with them he shall push the people together to the ends of the earth: and they are the ten thousands of Ephraim, and they are the thousands of Manasseh. Remember John Bull?*

6. *The Harp belongs to king David, well known for playing the harp and worship. 1 Samuel 16:14-23.*

7. *Dieu et mon droit* = *God and my right. Note that this kingdom acknowledges God. A lot of nations and governments do not. It also acknowledges that their rights come from God. A lot of governments do not. If it means my right hand there will be a sword in it and a sword is a symbol of Israel.*
8. *Mon droit* = *Benjamin: Genesis 35:18, Benjamin, Jacob's youngest son was called by Jacob:* **son of my right hand = Strongs 1144 =** בִּנְיָמִין
9. *Honi soit qui mal y pense* = *'Shame on him who thinks evil of it'* - *Most Noble Order of the Garter: This order of chivalry was founded by Edward 3 of England in 1348. He also claimed the French throne. It had habits and a belt.*

<u>Order of the Garter - Wikipedia</u>

10. *Now, compare this order to the prophets of the Old Testament. John the Baptist was the last of the Old Testament prophets. He was the greatest of them all because he baptized Jesus Christ in the Jordan river. Mark 1:9. He was clothed with* **camel's hair and a girdle of a skin about his loins.** *Mark 1:6. The Old Testament shows us spiritual things as examples of New Testament spiritual principles. 1 Corinthians 10:6-11.*
11. *When Jesus* **came up out of the water** *He was baptized with the Holy Ghost. Mark 1:8-10. For us it means we get baptized with The Holy Ghost and fire. Mathew 3:11-17. The fire is very real and like a cloak that sits heavily on your shoulders. Isaiah 9:5. It can make you run faster than a chariot. 1 Kings 18:46 and Acts 8:29-35.*
12. **You can also hitch a ride with an angel:**

39 And when they **were come up out of the water,** *the* **Spirit of the Lord caught away Philip,** *that the eunuch saw him no more: and he went on his way rejoicing.*

40 But **Philip was found at Azotus**: and passing through he preached in all the cities, till he came to Caesarea.

Acts 8:39-40. Saee also Ezekiel 1:3 and 2:2.

12 Then the spirit took me up, and I heard behind me a voice of a great rushing, (saying), Blessed be the glory of the Lord from his place. Ezekiel 3:12.

There is no "saying" in the original text.

Esechiel tells us how he went from Babylon to Jerusalem and back. Ezekiel 8:3

The point is **when The Holy Spirit Falls on you, things start happening very fast**: Mark 1:10 – straightway, verse 12: immediately, verse 18: straightaway, verse 20: straightaway, verse 21: straightaway, verse 28: immediately, verse 31: And he came and took her by the hand, and lifted her up; and **immediately** the fever left her, and she ministered unto them.

–8–

ASHER

Genesis 49:20

Deuteronomy 33:24-27
25 Thy shoes shall be iron and brass; and as thy days, so
shall thy strength be.

The biblical account introduces Asher, son of Jacob and Leah, with a narrative of prosperity and maritime engagement, revealing distinct attributes that define the tribe.

Asher's inheritance marked a coastal territory, hinting at possible maritime activities.

Collaboration with Dan, Naphtali, and Issachar in seafaring pursuits signifies Asher's maritime significance (Judges 5:17, Ezekiel 48:2-3, Joshua 17:10).

Blessings for Asher include happiness, dainties, and "feet dipped in oil," possibly indicating a connection to a region near the North Sea (Deuteronomy 33:24).

The Prophetess Deborah and Gideon's calls highlight Asher's involvement in maritime endeavors (Judges 5:17).

Yair Davidiy identifies Asher's potential presence in modern-day Ireland, linking them to Vandals and Burgundians.

The Burgundians, descendants of Beriah (Asher's son), may have contributed to populations in France and Germany.

Berea's association with Galatians, believed to have connections to Gaul's and Celts, emphasizes the ongoing dispersion of Israel (Acts 17:12).

Heraldic Emblems and Archaeological Clues:

Asher's heraldic symbols include images of happiness, royal dainties, and prosperity.

The mention of shoes of iron and brass aligns with artifacts found in Ireland, reinforcing a connection to Asher's biblical attributes. Deuteronomy 33:25

In summary, Asher's narrative blends biblical and historical elements, portraying a tribe deeply involved in maritime pursuits. The geographical, symbolic, and archaeological aspects contribute to a comprehensive understanding of Asher's enduring legacy throughout different epochs.

Notes by Author:

Deuteronomy 33:24-25

24 And of Asher he said, Let Asher be blessed with children; let him be acceptable to his brethren, and let him dip his foot in oil.
25 Thy shoes shall be iron and brass; and as thy days, so shall thy strength be.

My interpretation according to the Hebrew of verse 25 is: Iron and bronze shall be you sandals and your days shall be you as your strength.

Strongs 1270 = barzel: iron - בַּרְזֶל
Strongs 5178 = nechosheth: copper, bronze - נְחֹשֶׁת
Strongs 4515 = minal: a bolt – מִנְעָל.

I could not find any Heraldic coat of arms with Asher's combinations like ships together with oil and copper and bronze and iron and Danish dainties or things like that.
What I could find was the Tin Islands or Cassiterides which I assume included the British Isles.
See Cassiterides - Wikipedia

Early tin was produced from rich alluvial deposits, mainly found in West Cornwall, as well as St. Austell and Bodmin. Tin ore would be washed up into the moors and valleys and the ore extracted from there.
- William Rowland (william-rowland.com)

Why Tin? Tin was used to make copper alloys which had mechanical and corrosion resistant properties. Asher was found on ships and ships were used to carry Tin from the British mines to the Mediterranean and Eastern Metropoles. These alloys would be used with wood and iron to build ships as well.

The earliest use of steel was discovered in an Iron Age hill fort known as Broxmouth in East Lothian in the British Isles. Some iron artefacts can be dated to 490 – 375 BC. Made from high-carbon steel which had been deliberately heated and quenched in water, the artefacts are the earliest evidence of sophisticated blacksmithing skills in Britain.

Evidence of earliest steel use in Britain discovered (heritagedaily.com)

This is marvelous stuff in my mind: to think that they could manufacture high carbon steel at that time! It reminds me of a scripture I have read:

*13 And king Solomon sent and fetched Hiram out of Tyre. 14 He was a widow's son of **the tribe of Naphtali,** and his father was a man of Tyre, a worker in brass: and he was filled with wisdom, and understanding, and cunning to work all works in brass. And he came to king Solomon, and wrought all his work.*

So even in King Solomons time there were guys who knew all about working with these metals.

–9–

NAPHTALI

N aphtali, borne out of the complex dynamics between Rachel and Leah, emerges as a tribe with distinct characteristics and a rich heritage.

Born to Rachel through her maidservant Bilhah, Naphtali's name reflects the struggle associated with his birth (Gen 30:8).

The Hebrew term "naphtulim" embodies the essence of wrestling, encapsulating the challenges and striving nature of the tribe (Strongs 5319).

Jacob's blessing portrays **Naphtali as a deer set free,** symbolizing grace and liberation (Gen 49:21).

The reference to bearing beautiful fawns suggests fertility and a flourishing future.

Naphtali received an inheritance in the northern part of Israel. The tribe's territory included the Sea of Galilee, known for its natural beauty and fertility.

Despite Rachel's initial struggle for children, Naphtali becomes a representation of freedom and vitality.

The tribe's role in the conquest of Canaan under Joshua contributes to the historical narrative of Naphtali.

The wrestling spirit of Naphtali endures as part of the collective identity of the tribe, highlighting resilience and determination.

In essence, Naphtali's story is one of overcoming challenges and embracing freedom. The imagery of a deer set free and the struggles associated with its birth shape the narrative of a tribe marked by both resilience and a commitment to flourishing in their allotted inheritance.

Hosea 11:10

*They shall walk after the Lord: he shall **roar like a lion:** when he shall roar, then the children shall tremble from the west.*

In the prophetic verses of Hosea 11:10, a majestic image unfolds—a divine roar that reverberates from the west, echoing across the seas and continents. This profound proclamation carries significance that resonates through history and geography.

Hosea portrays the Lord roaring like a lion, a symbol of authority, power, and majesty. This divine roar signifies a significant intervention or proclamation.

The reference to the west encompasses the Mediterranean Sea and extends further to the Atlantic. This expansive view includes regions beyond, such as the Americas and South Africa.

Drawing a parallel with the bravery of Zebulun and Naphtali in Judges 5:18, a connection emerges. The courageous feats of their ancestor's hint at a shared heritage of bravery.

Zebulun and Naphtali fought side by side, jeopardizing their lives in the high places of the field during the time of Deborah and Barak. This camaraderie suggests a deep understanding and unity.

Isaiah's foresight in Isaiah 9:1-2 speaks of a glorious Light shining in the land of Zebulun and Naphtali. This Light is a profound revelation—Jesus Christ, the beacon of hope and salvation.

The bravery exhibited by Zebulun and Naphtali in ancient times seems to echo in the spirit of the Dutch and Norwegians, the descendants of these tribes, known for their courage and resilience.

In summary, Hosea's proclamation extends a divine roar from the west, echoing through time and geography. The bravery of

Zebulun and Naphtali becomes a timeless symbol, and Isaiah's vision adds a layer of spiritual significance with the advent of the Light. This prophetic imagery encapsulates the enduring spirit and connection across generations and continents.

Mathew 12:12-25

*Now when Jesus had heard that John was cast into prison, **he departed into Galilee;***

*And leaving Nazareth, he came and dwelt in **Capernaum, which is upon the sea coast, in the borders of Zabulon and Nephthalim:***

*That it might be fulfilled which was **spoken by Esaias the prophet,** saying,*

*The land of **Zabulon, and the land of Nephthalim,** by the **way of the sea,** beyond Jordan, **Galilee of the Gentiles;***

*The people which sat in darkness **saw great light;** and to them which sat in the region **and shadow of death** light is sprung up.*

***From that time Jesus began to preach,** and to say, repent: for the kingdom of heaven is at hand.*

And Jesus, walking by the sea of Galilee,** saw two brethren, Simon called Peter, and Andrew his brother, casting a net into the sea: for **they were fishers.

*And he saith unto them, **follow me, and I will make you fishers of men.***

*And they **straightway** left their nets, and followed him.*

And going on from thence, he saw other two brethren, James the son of Zebedee, and John his brother, in a ship with Zebedee their father, mending their nets; and he called them.

*And they **immediately** left the ship and their father, and followed him.*

*And Jesus went about **all Galilee, teaching in their synagogues,** and preaching the **gospel of the kingdom,** and healing all manner of sickness and all manner of disease among the people.*

*And his fame went throughout **all Syria:** and they brought unto him all sick people that were taken with divers diseases and torments, and those which were possessed with devils, and those which were lunatic, and those that had the palsy; and he healed them.*

*And there followed him great multitudes of people **from Galilee, and from Decapolis, and from Jerusalem, and from Judaea, and from beyond Jordan.***

Now I find some marvelously interesting things in this piece of scripture. First off, the Bible always follow the same protocol. We will always be referred back to the prophets and what they foretold us long ago. God always tells his prophets about it before it happens! Not to take note of the prophetic announcements can be pretty suicidal. Here we are referred back to Isaiah 9. After Jesus was baptized The Spirit of God (The Holy Spirit anointing) came on Him and was sent into the wilderness (remember when Israel was in the wilderness?) to be tested by Satan. Israel failed,

Jesus did not. Where does He go to? He goes to the Gentiles in the land of Zebulon and Naphtali! Are Zebulon and Naphtali Gentiles? Definitely not! They are genuine tribes from Israel! By the way exactly the same thing happened to Paul the Apostle. He went to the Gentiles. Were they from Israel or not? They were from Israel as we will prove throughout this book. In the exile they went and West through they Caucasian mountains and through Greece and Macedonia and west through Europe. Also West through the Mediterranean Sea and into Europe via Spain and Portugal and further to the British Isles. From there they went further West and South to New Amsterdam and the Cape of Good Hope and to the ends of the earth as per protocol. What protocol? The one Jesus and the Apostle Paul followed: first Jerusalem then Judea then Samaria then to the ends of the earth. Acts 1:8.

First the place was in darkness and Jesus turned the darkness into light. He chose his disciples from fishermen for a good reason; they were a seafaring people and they had to bring the Gospel to the nations. But they had to get schooling from the Greatest Rabbis of all time, Jesus Christ and The Holy Spirit and ye shall be witnesses unto Me according to the protocol; Jerusalem, Judea, Samaria and unto the uttermost part of the earth. Judea was where the Jews lived, Samaria was where Israel lived and then, only then to the rest of the world. Why? Because Israel was the anointed witness. But Israel was also the church. Why? Mathew 12:15 supplies the answer The land of **Zabulon, and the land of Nephthalim**, by the **way of the sea,** beyond Jordan, **Galilee of the Gentiles.** Israel became Gentiles after they got the letter (or certificate) of divorce from their previous husband, God Himself. They whored after other gods, physically and spiritually. To save them from their whoring ways God had no option but to take them out of those conditions and send them elsewhere. But He never abandoned them for all and sundry to destroy. He bought them back with the precious blood of his only begotten son Jesus Christ. Hosea 3:2. The price was established by the Jewish priests, as per the Law. (Thirty pieces of silver). Israel was warned to destroy the Canaanites who worshipped Baal and Ashtaroth. Off course they were also known by other names. Baal demanded child sacrifice and Ashera (Ashtaroth) demanded sexual liberties of all kinds. Hosea 2:8. Ahab and Jezebel drove this to a high. Hosea 5:3. And then the letter (or certificate) of divorce came. Deuteronomy 24:1, Hosea 2:1-2, Isaiah 50:1.

Authors Note: Dan and Zebulun and Naphtali (Dan's full brother) were always connected to the sea and ships.

Deuteronomy 33:23 [23] And of Naphtali he said, O Naphtali, satisfied with favour, and full with the blessing of the LORD: possess thou the west and the south.

Note this is a direct instruction, this is an order. There can be no ambiguity here! But west means sea in Hebrew: Strongs 3220: yam = sea – יָם

If Naphtali went west, he ran into the Mediterranean Sea. From there he had to tame the Atlantic Ocean to go south. This he did, together with Zebulun and Dan.

God cast them away they did listen to Him and they wandered among the nations. Hosea 9:17. But they will be called children of the living God. He will betroth Israel forever. Hos 2:19, Hosea 1:10. You cannot become a son of the living God but through Jesus Christ. So, Israel now became sons of the living God i.e. Christians. But they are from Israel none the less even if they are now not known as Israel and they are witnesses. Acts 1:8.

But ye shall receive power, after that the Holy Ghost is come upon you: and ye shall be witnesses unto me both in Jerusalem, and in all Judaea, and in Samaria, and unto the uttermost part of the earth.

The concept of witnesses encompasses both Israel, represented by the 12 tribes, and the Church—a theme echoing through the teachings of Jesus and the apostles.

Jesus addressed His words to Israel and the Menorah—the seven churches. The Menorah symbolizes the churches to whom the Apostle Paul preached, emphasizing his ministry to the Gentiles. But the symbol of the Menorah used in the book of Revelation belongs to the tabernacle of God as described by Moses for all of Israel. (see Exodus 25:31–37; 37:17–24). The geographical spread of Paul's teachings aligns with the divine protocol, reaching the ends of the earth.

Key scriptures emphasize the witness role of Israel and the Church. This includes Isaiah 43:10, where God designates Israel as His witnesses, and Matthew 28:19, instructing disciples to make witnesses of all nations. The requirement of two witnesses, as in Deuteronomy 19:15, underscores the significance of testimony.

Romans 1:16 outlines the protocol: the Gospel to the Jew first, then to the Greek (Gentile). This mirrors the divine sequence—Judea (Jews) followed by Samaria (Israel/Greeks). The dispersion among the Gentiles refers to Israel among the Greeks, reaffirming their witness role.

John 7:35 captures the question about Jesus teaching the dispersed among the Gentiles, with the term "Gentiles" denoting Hellēnōn or Greeks. However, these dispersed ones were the Israelites among the Greeks—a reality evident during the gatherings in Jerusalem on the day of Pentecost (Acts 2:5).

References to Naphtali's wisdom and understanding (1 Kings 7:14) align with his role among the tribes. Alongside Issachar and Zebulun, Naphtali was close to King David (1 Chron 12:40), reflecting a united purpose.

Zebulun and Naphtali were identified as seafaring nations in Isaiah 9:1 and affirmed in Matthew 12:15. The fishermen disciples, sent by Jesus, exemplify this, casting nets to catch men for the Kingdom. Their journey extends to the formation of New

Amsterdam (later New York) by the Dutch, who brought the Gospel.

The history of New York carries a transformative narrative. Despite the godly foundations laid by early settlers, the region faced moral challenges. Leaders like John D. Rockefeller failed to uphold righteous principles, contributing to the moral decline symbolized by the embrace of abortion.

In essence, the witnesses—Israel and the Church—unfold a dynamic narrative, testifying to the Gospel's transformative power. This journey involves geographic and spiritual dispersion, reflecting the divine protocol from Jerusalem to the ends of the earth.

Legalizing Abortions and Divine Warning

The controversial initiative to legalize abortions followed a predetermined trajectory, influenced significantly by a commission predominantly composed of pro-abortion advocates. In 1967, the chairman, John D. Rockefeller 3rd, a key figure in this development, received the prestigious Margaret Sanger Award from Planned Parenthood, notably, Margaret Sanger, the award's namesake, was the founder of Planned Parenthood, with a history marred by troubling associations with white supremacist ideologies.

A commission tasked with promoting abortion legalization exhibited a conspicuous bias in favor of pro-abortion stances. The appointment of individuals with such inclinations established the foundation for subsequent developments.

John D. Rockefeller 3rd, in his capacity as chairman, played a pivotal role in the commission. His acceptance of the Margaret Sanger Award from Planned Parenthood, an organization founded by a figure linked to white supremacist ideologies, introduced a controversial dimension to the unfolding events.

The decision to legalize abortions, considered contradictory to divine principles, encountered divine intervention. God's warning manifested dramatically on September 11, 2001, through the terrorist attacks on the Twin Towers. Children, observing the tragic events from a replica of the Halve Maen (Half Moon) on the Hudson River, sailed away as the towers crumbled.

For the leaders of this people cause them to err; and they that are led of them are destroyed. Isaiah 9:16

Authors Note: The first people that came to Manhattan Island were on a Dutch ship called Half Moon (Halve Maen). Halve Maen - Wikipedia. The captain was Henry Hudson, an Englishman commissioned by the Dutch East India Company. The Yacht, Halve Maen, went South West (remember Deuteronomy 33:23-25: possess thou the west and the south.) to reach Manhattan Island on September 11, 1609. The Dutch established a trading station there and called it New Amsterdam. They were Christians. Now fast forward to September 11, 2001. Children on a replica called Half Moon (Halve Maen) sail up the Hudson River to commemorate the landing of Henry Hudson on Manhattan Island on September 11, 1609. But they witness American Airlines Flight 11 and United Airlines Flight 175 fly into the Twin Towers and bring them down. Captain Chip Reynolds of the Half Moon saw the faces of the passengers on board the second plane and knew it was going to fly into the tower. From the Hudson: local crew of Half Moon Replica reflect on 9/11 | NEWS10 ABC

My contention is that it was a direct warning from God and that the reason for the "Finger of God" is to be found in the fact that the breach in the wall happened because of the abortion laws started by John D. Rockefeller 3 in New York on April 1970. How a Jewish legislator's vote legalized abortion in New York in 1970 – The Forward
The moon went through 50% during the night and that to me is the finger of God. Moon Phase on September 11, 2001 (moongiant.com)
Psalms 89:37 KJV: It shall be established for ever as the moon, and as a faithful witness in heaven.

Timeline of the September 11 Attacks | Britannica

Do we dare look at the flight paths and their origins for clues as to the Finger of God? For instance:

- *2 fingers from Boston – City of Light on the Hill? City upon a Hill - Wikipedia*
- *New York City to Shanksville – self destruction?*
- *Washington to Washington – self destruction?*
- *Killing your own children equals self- destruction. That, is what Baal worship expected.*

This is the Finger of God

- *Exodus 8:19 KJV*
- *John 8:6, 8*
- *Luke 11:20 KJV*

The juxtaposition of the push for abortion legalization with divine intervention underscores the gravity of the situation. The acknowledgment of God's disapproval, symbolized by the dramatic events of 9/11, serves as a sobering reflection on the moral choices made by society.

Coat of Arms of Northern Ireland - Coat of arms of Northern Ireland - Wikipedia.

Notes:

1. *Stag = Naphtali Genesis 49:21*
2. *Lion = Israel, Judah, Dan, Gad. Genesis 49:9*
3. *Red Cross = Christian cross*
4. *Harp = King David's harp. 1 Samuel 16:14-23*
5. *Crown = Kingdom of Israel Revelation 1:6, 5:10.*
6. *Red Hand = Refers to Judah and Tamar's 2nd son (Zarah) born with the scarlet thread around his wrist. Genesis 38:27-30*

–10–

JOSEPH

Genesis 30:22-24

*And God remembered Rachel, and God hearkened to her,
and opened her womb.
And she conceived, and bare a son; and said, God hath
taken away my reproach:
And she called his name Joseph; and said, The Lord shall
add to me another son.*

In Genesis 30:22-24, the birth of Joseph is marked by divine favor. Rachel, who had longed for children, joyfully exclaimed that God had taken away her reproach, naming her son Joseph, which means "God will add." The fulfillment of this name is evident not only in the birth of Manasseh but also in the abundant blessings bestowed upon the descendants of Joseph.

Jacob's prophetic blessing in Genesis 49:22-46 portrays Joseph as a fruitful bough by a well, with branches extending over the wall. Though archers shot at him, Joseph overcame, strengthened by the God of Abraham, Isaac, and Jacob. The blessings encompassed fruitful offspring, symbolized by the fruit of the womb. Ephraim, a significant tribe of Joseph, played a massive role in Israel's history and continues to do so in Great Britain and the USA. Manasseh, the eldest, finds representation in the UK, while Ephraim, the youngest and most populous, aligns with the USA, fulfilling Jacob's prophecy in Genesis 48:19.

In the Great Seal of the United States, the symbolism becomes apparent, reflecting the unity of all Israelite tribes through Ephraim and Manasseh. Thirteen stars and other elements denote the inclusion of all the tribes in Ephraim, with Juda (the Jews) represented separately. This unity is echoed in Ezekiel 37:16, where the sticks come together in the hand of the Great Eagle on the seal.

Moses, in Deuteronomy 33:13-17, reiterates the blessings upon Joseph, emphasizing abundance from heaven, earth, and sea. Notably, the unicorn, symbolizing Joseph and Israel, is present in the Royal Coat of Arms of the UK. The unicorn's connection with the USA is evident, considering the migration of a significant number of UK inhabitants to America. The unicorn represents Joseph, and the fruitful bough, along with arrows, is embodied in the Great Seal of the USA.

The historical and heraldic symbols serve as a testament to the enduring significance of Joseph's name, embodying the idea that God will add blessings and prosperity to His people.

Author's note: Refer to Great seal of the USA above.

–11–

BENJAMIN

In Genesis 35:18, Benjamin, Jacob's youngest son, received his name from his grieving mother Rachel. Initially named Benoni, meaning "son of my sorrow," his father Jacob renamed him Benjamin, signifying "son of my right hand" or "son of my days." Being the youngest and the son of Jacob's beloved wife, Rachel, Benjamin held a special place in Jacob's heart.

Jacob's prophetic blessing in **Genesis 49:27** described **Benjamin as a ravenous wolf**. This imagery depicted his prowess in battle, devouring prey in the morning and dividing the spoil at night. Moses, in Deuteronomy 33:12, further prophesied that Benjamin would be the beloved of Yahweh, kept safe throughout the day and carried by God between His shoulders.

Benjamin's tribe faced a critical moment during the time of the Judges, where their exceptional skills in battle led to near annihilation. A grave incident in Gibeah involving the abuse and death of a Levite's concubine ignited a severe conflict. Benjamin, protecting the perpetrators, resisted the calls for justice from the other tribes. The resulting warfare led to the loss of thousands of Benjamin's men, with only 600 survivors retreating to the wilderness.

The gravity of this situation prompts reflection on the moral state of society during that period. Conditions akin to those in Sodom and Gomorrah or the time of Noah prevailed, with extreme moral decay and violence. God's sanctioning of the tribes near extinction serves as a solemn reminder of divine judgment on unrepentant sin.

The association of Benjamin with symbols such as the wolf, sword, bow, arrows, and highlights the tribe's strength and warrior prowess. Despite the challenging circumstances, Benjamin's survival ultimately depended on God's intervention and the collective repentance of the other tribes.

King Saul, a notable figure from Benjamin, initially did well until he turned to the occult. The Apostle Saul (Paul) also hailed from the tribe of Benjamin, highlighting the tribe's diverse historical contributions.

In contemporary times, the call for repentance and reflection arises, considering societal issues such as the LGBTQ movement and the ethical concerns surrounding abortion. The prophetic symbols of Benjamin may serve as a stark reminder of the importance of moral choices and the potential consequences of societal drift from divine principles.

Wolf Pack

This was the emblem of the 12th Combat Flotilla in Bordeaux under KrvKpt. Klaus Scholz in Oct. 1942. They operated the milch cows and other long - range boats.

Emblems - German U-boats of WWII - Kriegsmarine - uboat.net

This Coat of Arms is in the Public Domain.

The 12 tribes in Revelation

Revelation 21:12

Joseph is mentioned in Revelation 7 verse 8 for 12 000 and his son Manasseh is also mentioned for 12 000 in verse 6. Now interestingly enough Ephraim the son of Joseph is mentioned countless times in the Old - testament as representing Israel the Northern Kingdom. Now why would an important person like Ephraim be overlooked? Let us look at what Jacob himself had to say?

In exploring the symbols associated with Ephraim and Manasseh, we uncover profound emblems deeply ingrained in the historical and heraldic legacy of Israel. As documented in Genesis 48:22, Jacob, also known as Israel, imparts blessings upon Ephraim and Manasseh, embracing them as his own sons. These blessings introduce enduring symbols that resonate across the tribes of Israel, particularly within the contemporary landscapes of the United Kingdom and the United States.

The symbolism of the sword, bow, and arrows originates from Jacob's prophetic blessings in Genesis 48:22. These emblems symbolize strength, unity, and military prowess, reflecting the rich heritage of Ephraim and Manasseh. Beyond these two tribes, these symbols permeate the broader heraldic emblems of all the tribes of Israel.

Ephraim, representing a multitude of nations, mirrors the diverse impact of the tribe. This aligns seamlessly with the cultural diversity of the United States, where various ethnicities converge. Ephraim's symbolism as a unifying force: echoes in the mosaic of backgrounds present in the U.S. On the other hand, Manasseh, as the elder brother, finds resonance in the United Kingdom, while the USA, as the younger brother, has emerged as a global force. The interplay of these symbols underscores the intricate historical connections and shared heritage between the UK and the USA.

A pivotal emblem, the majestic eagle, graces the Great Seal of the United States, bearing the symbols of Joseph—Ephraim and Manasseh—in its grasp. This powerful imagery signifies the enduring impact of Joseph's descendants on the nation's identity and values. The outstretched wings of the eagle embody strength, liberty, and resilience, embodying the essence of the tribes' influence.

Exploring the German origins and migration to the USA unveils the continued significance of the eagle symbol. German immigrants brought this emblem, establishing a tangible link between the old world and the new. The adoption of the eagle symbol by German-descendant communities in the USA serves as a testament to the lasting impact of ancestral symbols.

In summary, the symbols of Ephraim and Manasseh transcend their historical roots, resonating in the heraldic emblems of Israel and finding vivid expression in the contemporary identities of the United Kingdom and the United States. The interweaving of these symbols reflects the enduring legacy of the tribes of Israel, exerting a profound influence on the cultural fabric of these nations.

In unraveling the symbolism woven into the annals of history, the double-headed eagle is a prominent emblem, not exclusive to Germany but rooted in the coat of arms of Rome and the Holy Roman Empire. A notable representation can be found in the Coat of Arms of the Holy Roman Empire, depicted in a 1540s manuscript by Virgil Solis.

The double-headed eagle, reminiscent of the two-faced god Janus, invokes a connection between Roman and Holy Roman Empire symbolism. Janus, showcased in the Vatican Museum, signifies transitions, doors, and passages, aligning with the historical shifts represented by the double-headed eagle.

In the context of Israel's tribes, Rachel's adoption of Dan

and his brother Naphtali is notable (Genesis 30:6). Dan's role as a judge among his people is prophesied by Jacob (Genesis 49:16) and reiterated in subsequent scriptures (Exodus 31:6, Deuteronomy 33:22, Joshua 19:47).

Collaborations between Dan, Ephraim, and Manasseh are evident in historical accounts (Jeremiah 4:15, Joshua 21:5).

Although Dan was the second largest tribe in Israel, their allotted land in the Philistine territory was insufficient. This led them north, where they acquired seafaring skills from the Phoenicians, particularly Tyros and Sidon.

The influence of idol worship during this period is acknowledged, yet Dan eventually outgrew it as they embarked on maritime expeditions, sailing westward.

Denmark, etymologically linked to Dan, stands as a lasting testament to their historical presence and influence.

Die Zuid Afrikaansche Republiek

The flag comparison between the old South African Republics, Israel, and the USA unveils intricate threads connecting these nations through symbolism, manifesting the enduring legacy of Dan's exploratory journeys.

Coat of Arms of the Republic of Transvaal around the 1900s.

Coat of arms of the Transvaal - Wikipedia

"Dit het vir net minder as 50 jaar bestaan en het in 1902 tot 'n einde gekom nadat Brittanje die republiek in die Tweede Vryheidsoorlog (ook bekend as die Anglo-Boereoorlog) verslaan het." – In Afrikaans.

Notes:

1. Eagle= Tribe of Dan (North)
2. Lion = Tribe of Judah (East)
3. Ox wagon = Tribe of Ephraim (bullock)(West)
4. Man = Tribe of Reuben (South)
5. Remember each leader lead 3 tribes making 12 in all. Just like the breastplate. Isaiah 59:17, Ephesians 6:14 and Exodus 25:7 (Ephod and Breastplate).
6. Anchor = seafaring people
7. Eendragt maakt magt = Unity makes strength
8. Compare to E pluribus unum.

Ezekiel 37:15-17

15 The word of the Lord came again unto me, saying,

16 Moreover, thou son of man, take thee one stick, and write upon it, For Judah, and for the children of Israel his companions: then take another stick, and write upon it, For Joseph, the stick of Ephraim and for all the house of Israel his companions:

17 And join them one to another into one stick; and they shall become one in thine hand.

As we delve into the rich tapestry of symbols, the interplay between historical emblems and biblical prophecies unfolds, revealing a multifaceted narrative that transcends geographical boundaries.

The lion, a powerful emblem entrenched in the UK's Royal Coat of Arms, symbolizes strength and royalty. Notably, it has ties to the tribes of Judah, Dan, and Gad, as depicted in Deuteronomy

33. This symbolic convergence underscores the multifaceted nature of historical emblems.

Gad and Goth, entwined in linguistic threads, echo through history. The House of Saxe-Coburg and Gotha, linked to British rulers, draws connections to Anglo-Saxons and Goths. The exploration of linguistic nuances, including the transformation of the Dalet sound from "D" to a "Th" sound, adds depth to our understanding of historical pronunciations.

The historical pronunciation of the Dalet, marked by a dot (dagesh), unveils a shift from the modern English "D" to a more "Th" sound. This linguistic evolution reflects the fluidity of language and highlights the nuanced aspects of pronunciation over time.

As we navigate the intricate tapestry of linguistic shifts and symbolic representations, the echoes of Gad, Goth, and the lion resound across historical landscapes. The convergence of biblical imagery and historical titles fosters a deeper appreciation for the interconnectedness of nations and the diverse threads woven into their identities.

In the sacred fabric of biblical visions, Ezekiel unveils a majestic scene where cherubim, celestial beings with multiple faces, stand as guardians before the throne of God. Cherubim, referring to more than one cherub in Hebrew, play a crucial role in Israel's spiritual heritage.

Ezekiel, in awe of the divine presence, describes the cherubim with faces symbolizing profound attributes. To the north, the face of an eagle; to the east, the face of a lion; to the south, the face of a man; and to the west, the face of a bullock. These symbols resonate with deep spiritual significance.

From the inception of Israel, cherubim served as protectors, facing the mercy seat where the blood of Jesus Christ symbolically resided. Exodus 37:8 highlights their presence, emphasizing the covenant's eternal nature, guarded by these celestial beings.

The Ark of the Covenant, adorned with cherubim, embodies

a profound truth. When Israel and their king invoke the covenant with Abraham, Isaac, Jacob, and King David, the cherubim watch over the mercy seat, signifying God's enduring commitment to His people.

The New Testament unveils the transformation of a cherub into a roaring lion, depicting Satan's fall. As described in 1 Peter 5:8, Satan prowls like a roaring lion, seeking whom he may devour. The cherub's face resembling a lion echo in this ominous symbolism.

Revelation 4:7 unveils a similar vision of celestial beings—cherubim—with faces like a lion, a calf, a man, and a flying eagle. John the Revelator, writing in veiled language to elude Roman scrutiny, captures the essence of Ezekiel's celestial journey.

Ezekiel's encounter with the cherubim becomes a timeless testament to God's covenant, protection, and the unfolding celestial drama revealed in Revelation. The cherubim, with faces symbolizing majesty and strength, stand as sentinels over the covenant, urging humanity to seek refuge under the wings of divine protection.

Ezekiel, a prophet of profound visions, embarked on extraordinary journeys in the celestial realm, providing glimpses into the spiritual tapestry of his time. His encounters, as documented in Ezekiel 8:3 and 11:1, reveal celestial machinery guided by magnetic forces, lifting him between earth and heaven.

In Ezekiel 8:3, the prophet experiences an otherworldly ascent, lifted by the Spirit of God into the visions of God. Transported to Jerusalem, Ezekiel witnesses the seat of the image of jealousy, provoking divine ire.

Ezekiel 11:1 unfolds another celestial journey, this time to the east gate of the Lord's house. Here, Ezekiel confronts idolatry as leaders, including Jaazaniah and Pelatiah, indulge in sun worship, symbolized by their focus on the rising sun in the east.

A surprising twist occurs as Ezekiel encounters Satan, who, being a fallen cherub, masquerades as an angel of light. This transformation, detailed in 2 Corinthians 11:14, underscores Satan's deceptive tactics, masquerading amidst the very people he once belonged to.

Ezekiel 28:14-19 unravels Satan's tragic fall from grace. Once the anointed cherub that covered the holy realm, Satan succumbed to profanity, corruption, and violence. His wings, akin to those on the Ark of the Covenant, will be clipped as he crashes and burns in divine judgment.

The conclusion brings forth the vibrancy of Israel's existence, transcending mere nomenclature. Now recognized as Sons of the Living God, as prophesied in Hosea 1:10 and Romans 9:26, Israel continues to lead nations, fulfilling the covenant with Abraham, Isaac, and Jacob.

Ezekiel's celestial journeys unravel a cosmic drama where divine revelations expose idolatry, deceit, and the ultimate destiny of celestial beings. As the celestial machinery orchestrates these visions, the enduring legacy of Israel, now Sons of the Living God, remains a testament to the fulfillment of God's promises.

Witnesses

> 10 **Ye are my witnesses**, saith the Lord, and my servant whom I have chosen: that ye may know and believe me, and understand that I am he: before me there was no God formed, neither shall there be after me.

> 11 I, even I, am the Lord; and beside me there is no savior.

> **Isaiah 43:10-11**

> 3 And I will give power unto **my two witnesses**, and they shall prophesy a thousand two hundred and threescore days, clothed in sackcloth.

Revelations 11:3

If you want to become a witness, just say to Jesus: "Please save me now". You will be saved. Romans 10:9

9 That if thou shalt confess with thy mouth the Lord Jesus, and shalt believe in thine heart that God hath raised him from the dead, thou shalt be saved.

The man that was crucified with Jesus did it and was saved in the nick of time: Luke 23:42-43.

–12–

EPHRAIM

In Revelation 7 we find all the tribes listed by name and the fullness they represent. Therefore, we can see God wants us to understand that it is the tribes of Israel and nobody else that He is referring to. The 7 churches are something else. There are letters written to each one specifically as well. There is a real difference between the body of Christ and the bride of Christ. But Ephraim and Dan are not mentioned in this list! But why? They were two very big tribes and leaders of the Western and Northern tribes as they camped in the wilderness. Also, Ephraim represent all the Northern tribes all the time in the Old Testament. Numbers 2:18, Isaiah 9:21. So why did he disappear? The reason lies beforehand. Ephraim and Manasseh are children of Joseph and they were adopted by Jacob as his own children in Genesis 48:5 "And now thy two sons, Ephraim and Manasseh, which were born unto thee in the land of Egypt before I came unto thee into Egypt, *are* mine; as Reuben and Simeon, they shall be mine." This makes 13 tribes. But there are only 12 mentioned in Revelation and 2 of them are Joseph and Manasseh. But Ephraim and Manasseh are Joseph's sons. But as we have seen Ephraim actually represented all of Israel. Dan thus remain as the only tribe not specifically mentioned in Revelation. What happened to Dan? He should be very visible as a judge among his people, Dan means judge. I believe the Tribe of Dan went before all the other tribes into Europe and the UK and the US and South Africa and the rest of the world as a sea faring nation. Judges 5:17:- "Gilead abode beyond Jordan: and why did Dan remain in ships? Asher continued on the sea shore, and abode in his breaches." As we have seen above the name of Dan can be traced all over Europe and the UK. The symbol of Dan was the Eagle and the Eagle can be seen very prominently on the Great Seal of the US. Therefore I submit that Dan was assimilated into all the tribes of the West as can be derived from his name and symbols.

ABOUT THE AUTHOR

Johan Andreas Rautenbach was born in Kroonstad in the Orange Free State of South Africa and grew up on a farm near Kroonstad. The family used to have a Friesland Dairy farm and grew crops mostly for the dairy cows and bulls which were sold to other Friesland studs. He went to primary school in Kroonstad and High School in Central High School in Bloemfontein, the Capital of the Free State. After High school he went to University (College) which was then called Potchefstroom University for Christian Higher Education. Today it is called North - West University. The course was called B. Comm. and the main subjects were Accounting and Business Economics and South African and Dutch and Roman Law. Other subjects were English and German and International Law and so on. He also did a Postgraduate management course at Pretoria University. He started off as an accountant in the family business and went on to become Managing Director in one of the Group's branches. The third generation of the family lost interest in the business and everything was sold lock stock and barrel. Andre now had to find a new direction in occupation and turned to Mechanical and Electrical projects. In this process he became a Millwright and Mechanical Engineer. The last project he was involved in was called the Majuba Rail Project, which involved building a 68 km railroad to the Majuba Power Station for supplying coal the Power Station for burning coal in the huge boilers. That equals to about 14 million tons of coal per annum. This produced steam to drive massive turbines which in turn drove massive generators to produce much needed electricity for the South African electrical grid. After this Andre took a sabbatical of 7 years to write a series of 7 books called A Third of the Submarines in the sea died, The Lost 13 Tribes of Israel, Apocalypsis and others.